THE WORM

For Marie,
my little silkworm

Originally published as *Le ver* by Les éditions de la courte échelle inc.

Copyright © 2014 Elise Gravel
Copyright for the French edition: Elise Gravel and Les éditions de la courte échelle inc., 2012

Published in Canada by Tundra Books, a division of Random House of Canada Limited,
One Toronto Street, Suite 300, Toronto, Ontario M5C 2V6

Published in the United States by Tundra Books of Northern New York,
P.O. Box 1030, Plattsburgh, New York 12901

Library of Congress Control Number: 2013940757

Library and Archives Canada Cataloguing in Publication

Gravel, Elise
[Ver. English]
        The worm / written and illustrated by Elise Gravel.

(Disgusting critters)
Translation of: Le ver.
Issued in print and electronic formats.
ISBN 978-1-77049-633-0 (bound).—ISBN 978-1-77049-635-4 (epub)

        I. Worms—Juvenile literature. I. Title. II. Title: Ver. English.

QL386.6.G7213 2014   j592'.3   C2013-903537-0

English edition edited by Samantha Swenson
Designed by Elise Gravel and Tundra Books
The artwork in this book was rendered digitally.

www.tundrabooks.com

Printed and bound in China

1 2 3 4 5 6   19 18 17 16 15 14

Elise Gravel
THE WORM

OH, HI!

Tundra Books

LADIES AND GENTLEMEN,

I present to you

THE WORM.

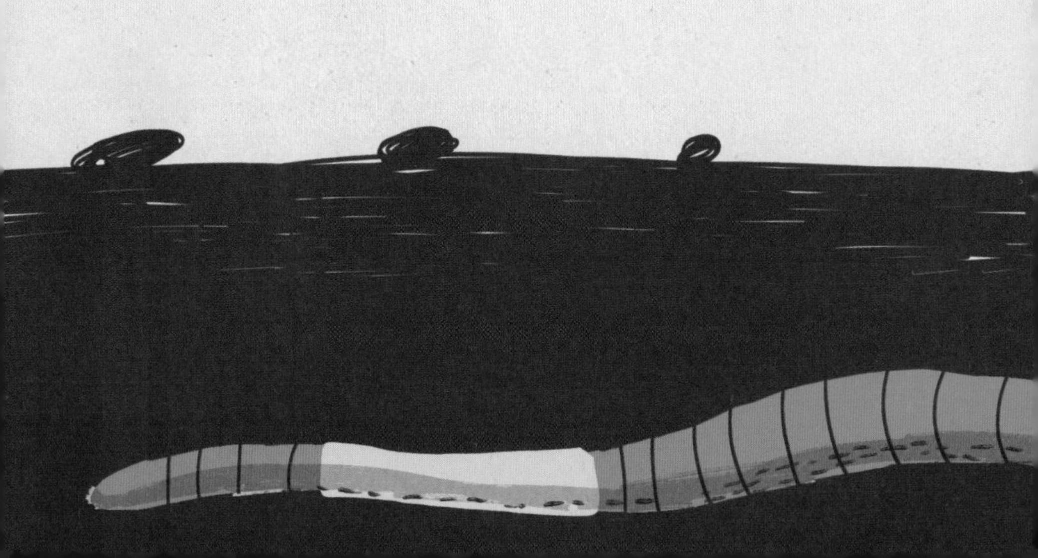

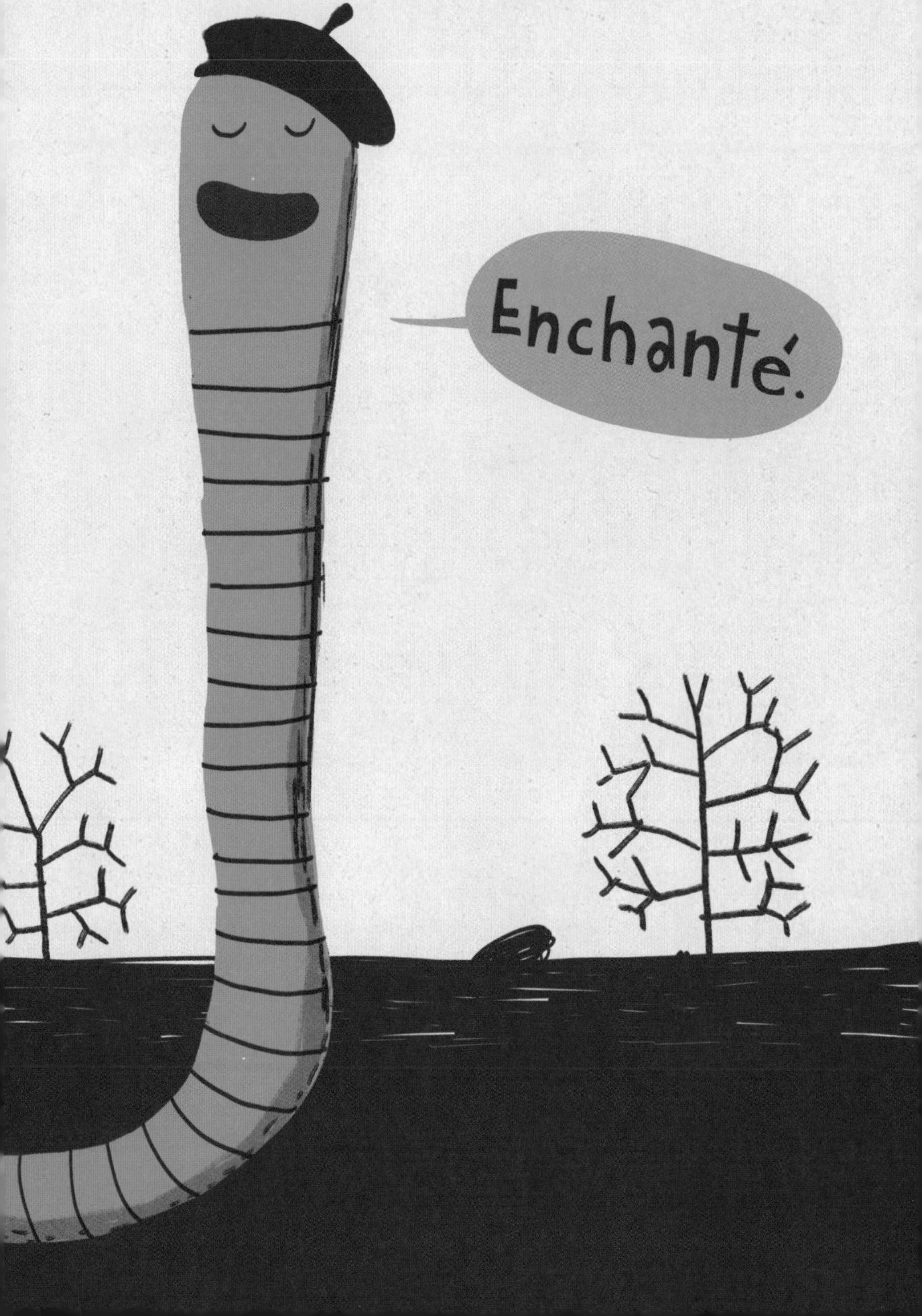
Enchanté.

The worm is a long animal that's shaped like a tube. It doesn't have a

SKELETON

or a spine: it's an

INVERTEBRATE.

It also doesn't have any legs.

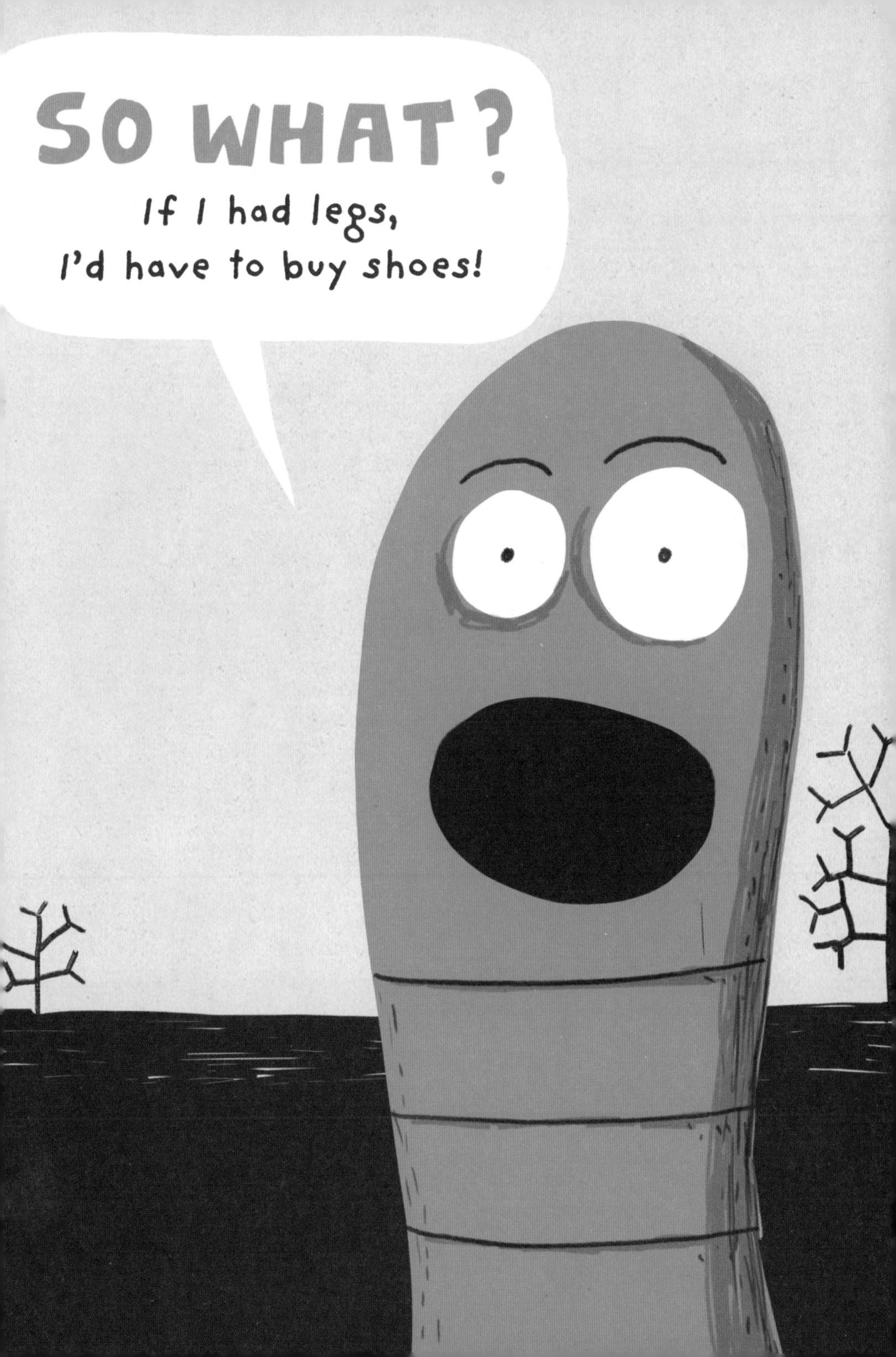
SO WHAT?
If I had legs,
I'd have to buy shoes!

There are many

DIFFERENT

kinds of worms.

HERE ARE SOME OF THEM:

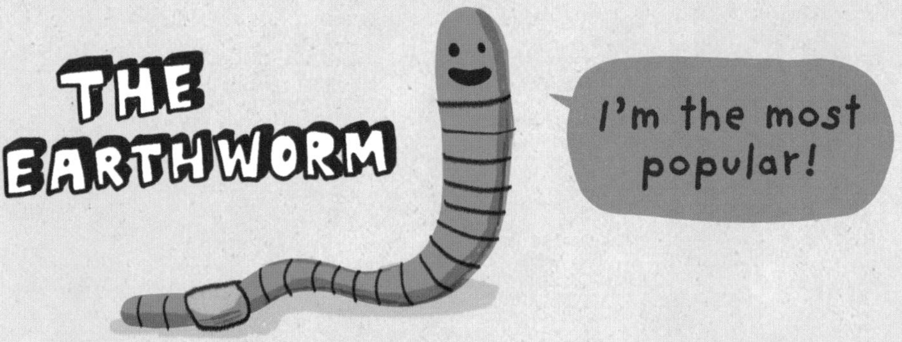
THE EARTHWORM
I'm the most popular!

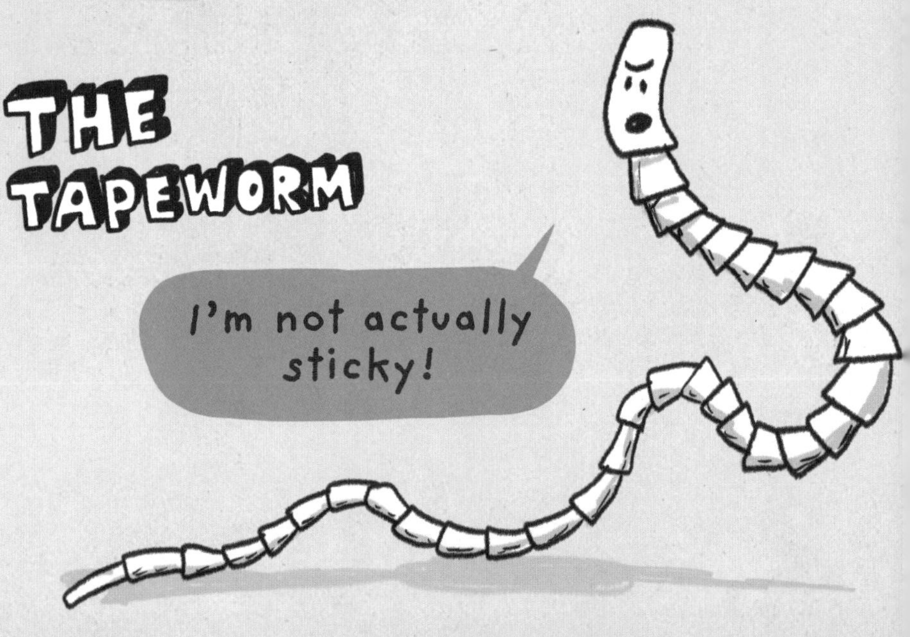
THE TAPEWORM
I'm not actually sticky!

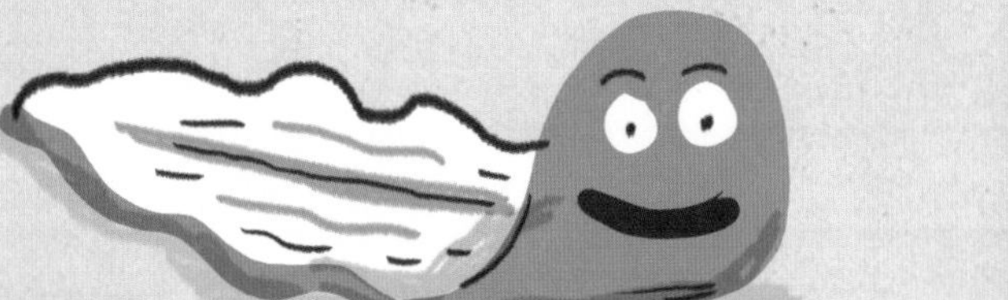

THE FLATWORM

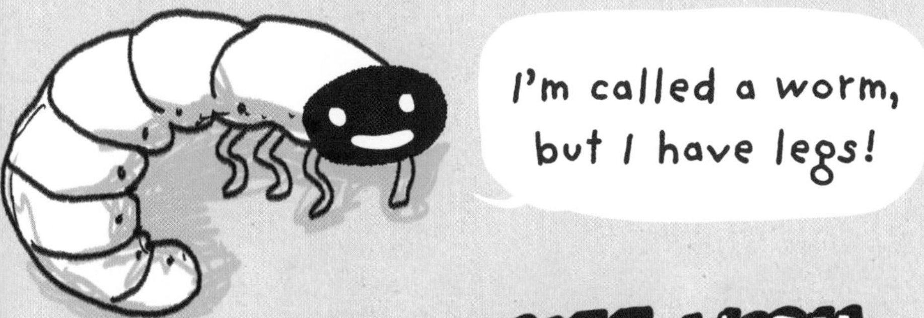
I'm called a worm, but I have legs!

THE WHITE WORM

Many insect larvae,
like

THE MAGGOT

(baby fly)

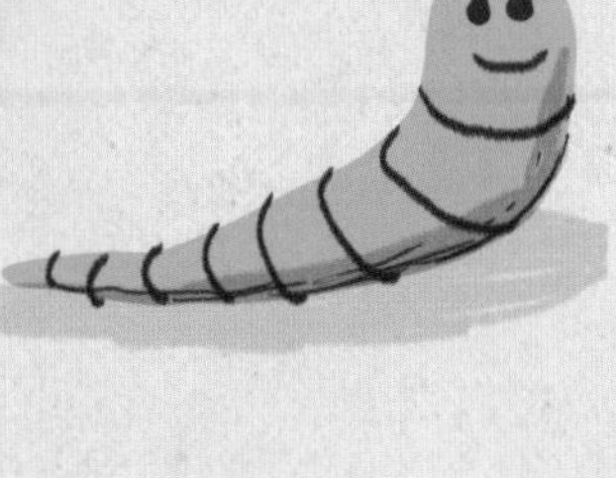

Some worms are so small that you need a microscope to see them. Others can be 115 feet (35 meters) long, like the ribbon worm that lives in oceans and rivers.

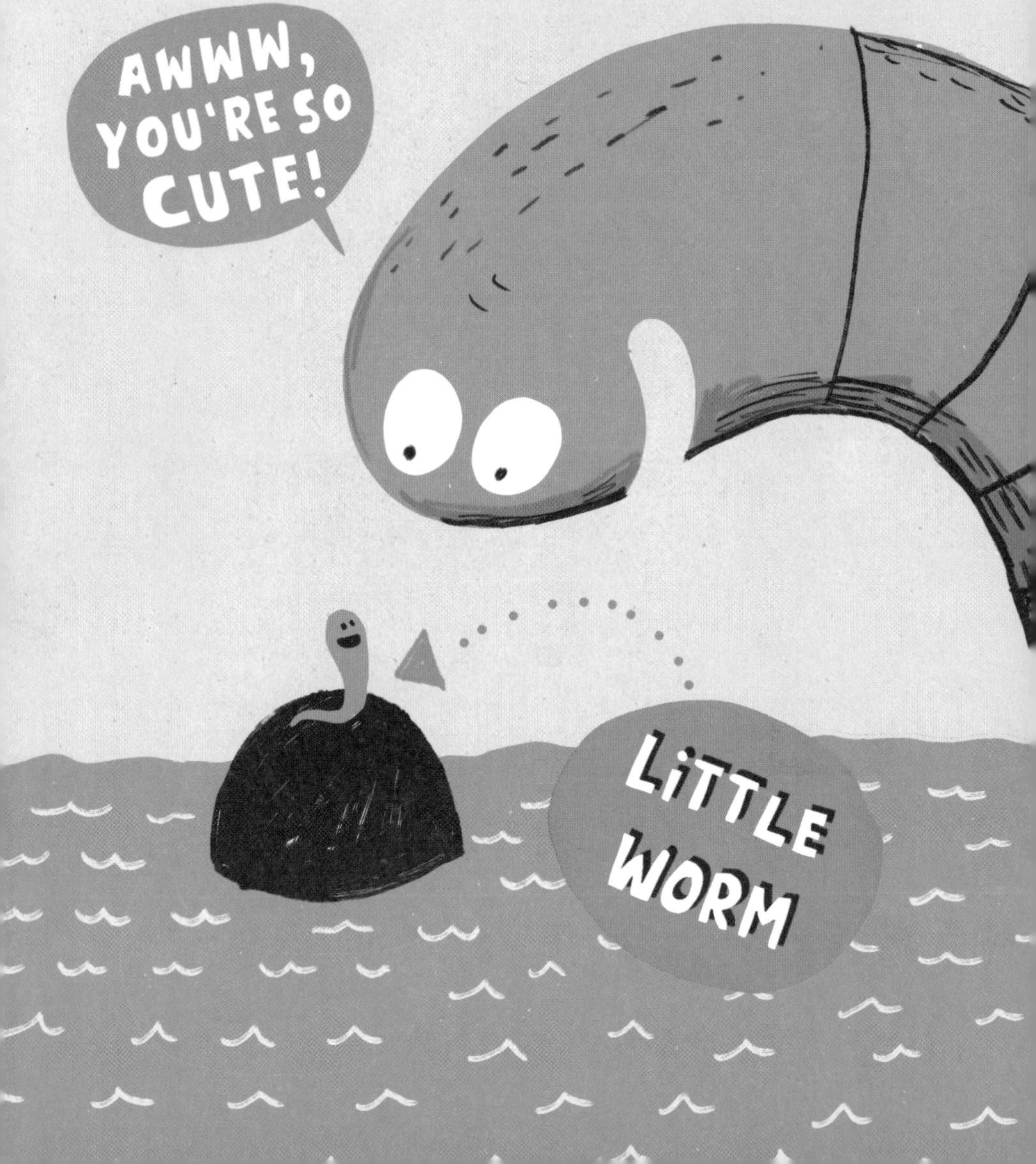
AWWW, YOU'RE SO CUTE!
LITTLE WORM

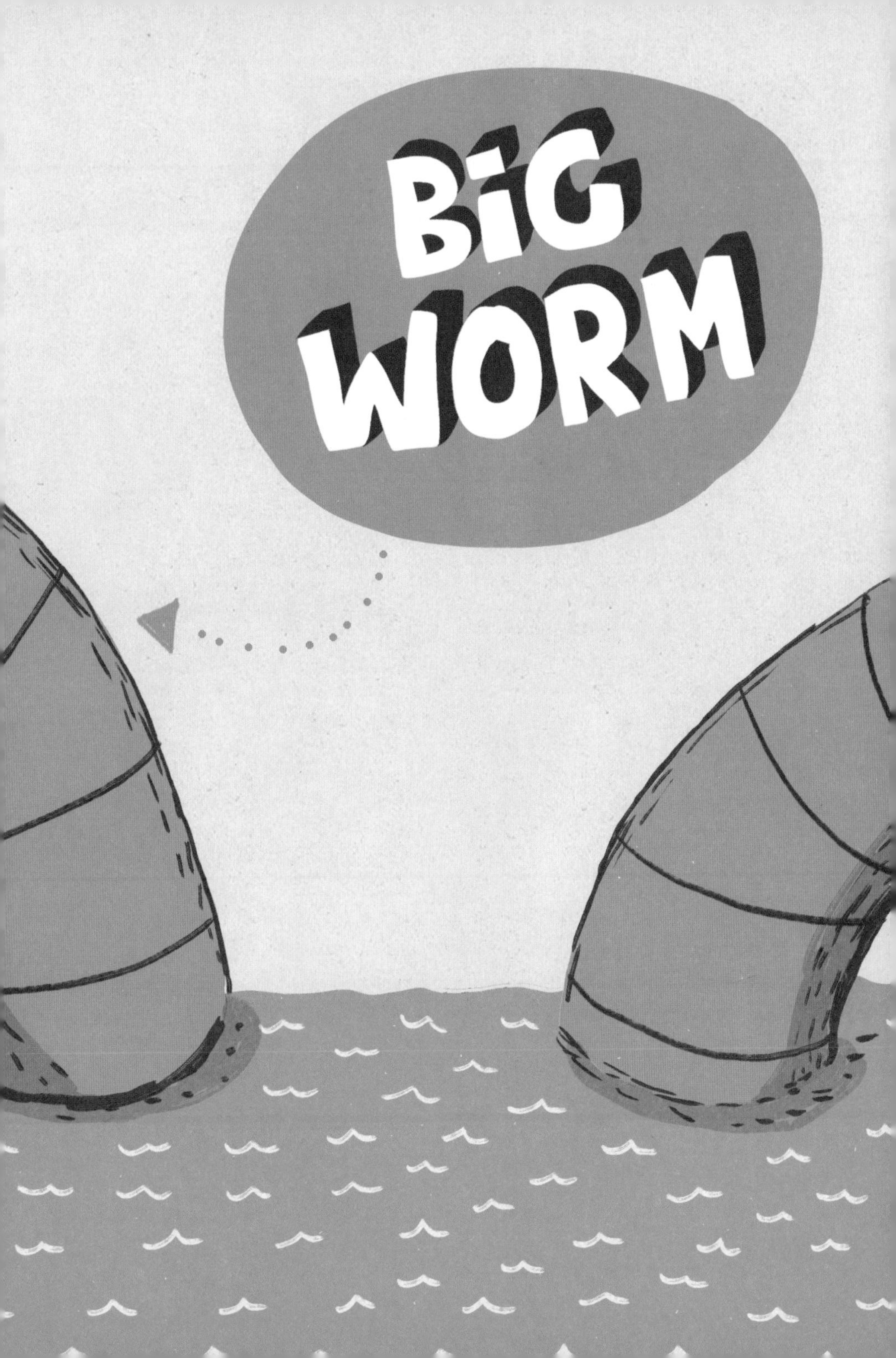
BIG
WORM

Worms can live in different

HABITATS.

Some live in the water. Others live in rotting plants. Some even live inside human or animal bodies!

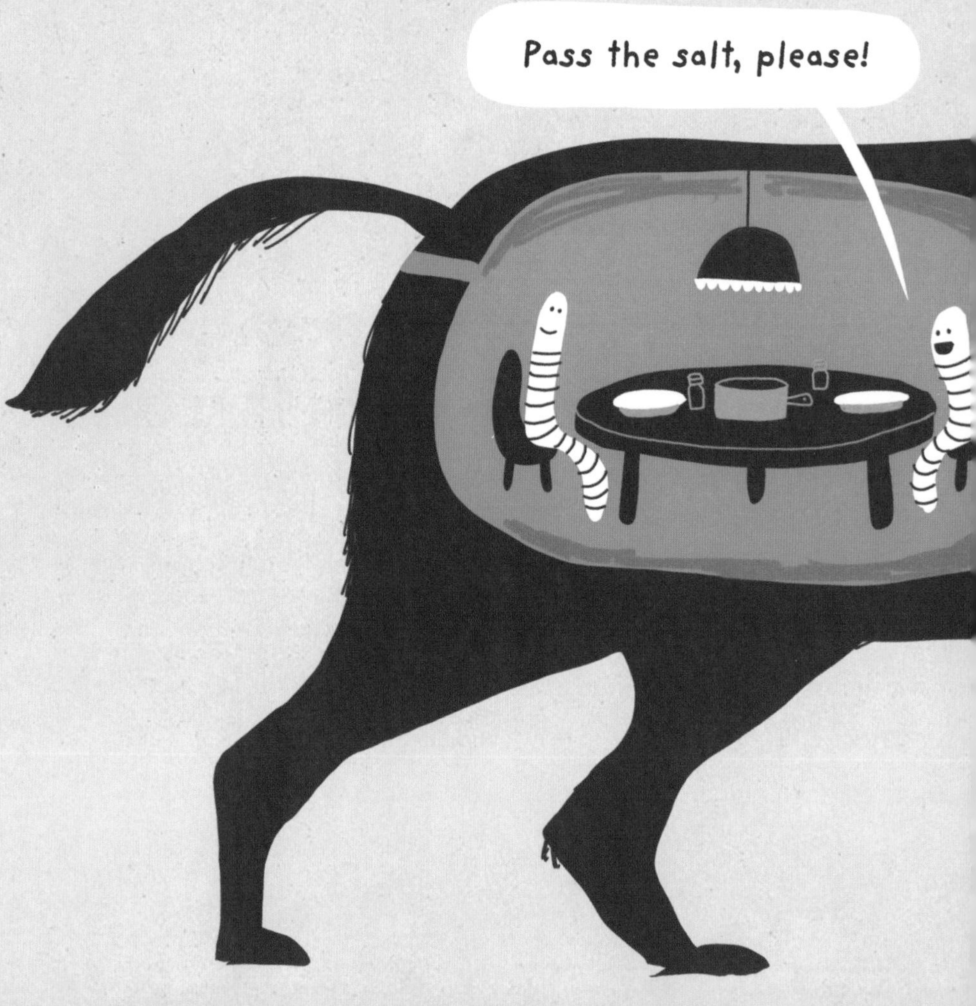
Pass the salt, please!

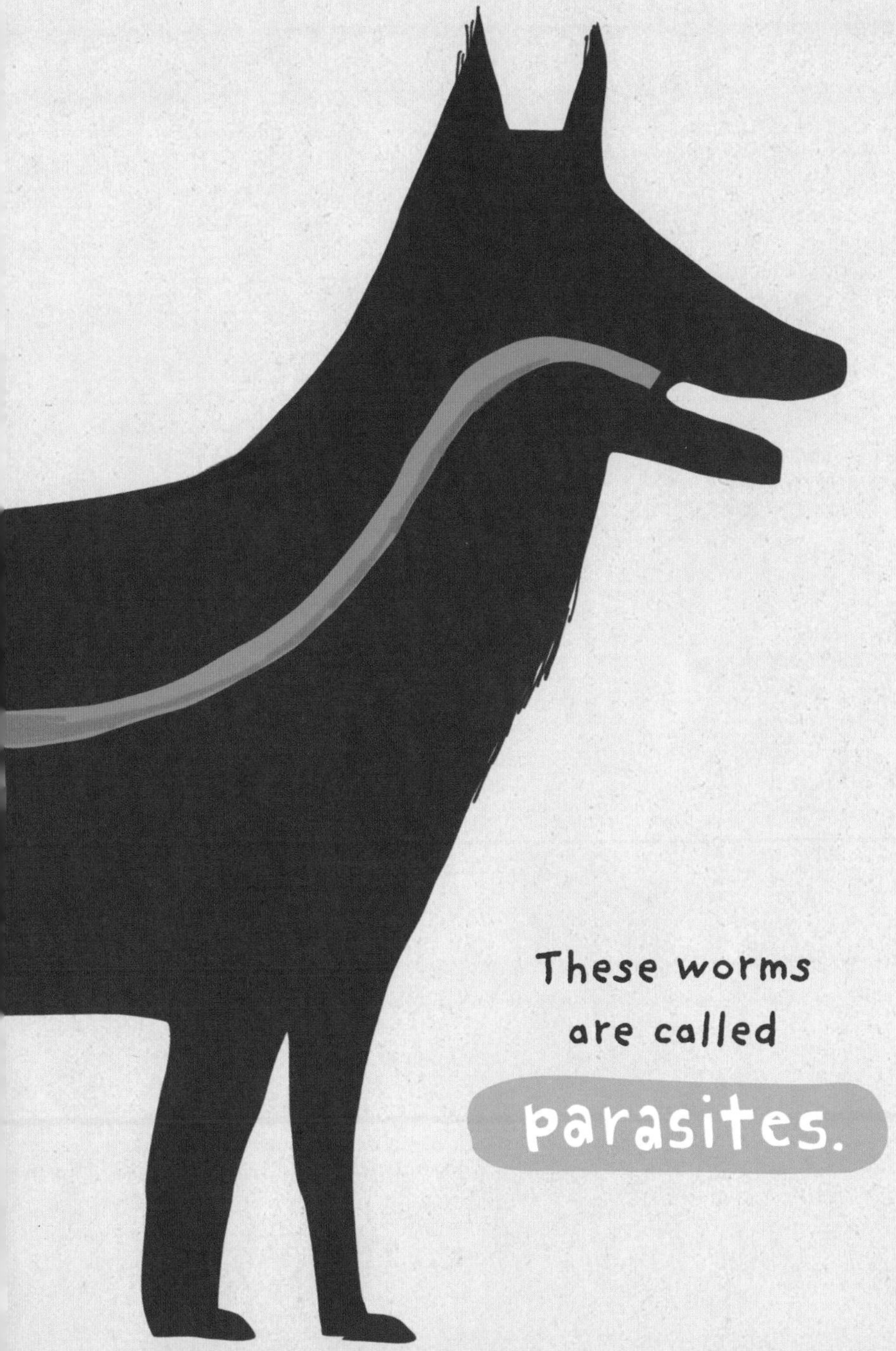

These worms
are called
parasites.

The most common worm is the

EARTHWORM.

An earthworm is basically a long

DIGESTIVE TRACT

inside a

MUSCLE TUBE.

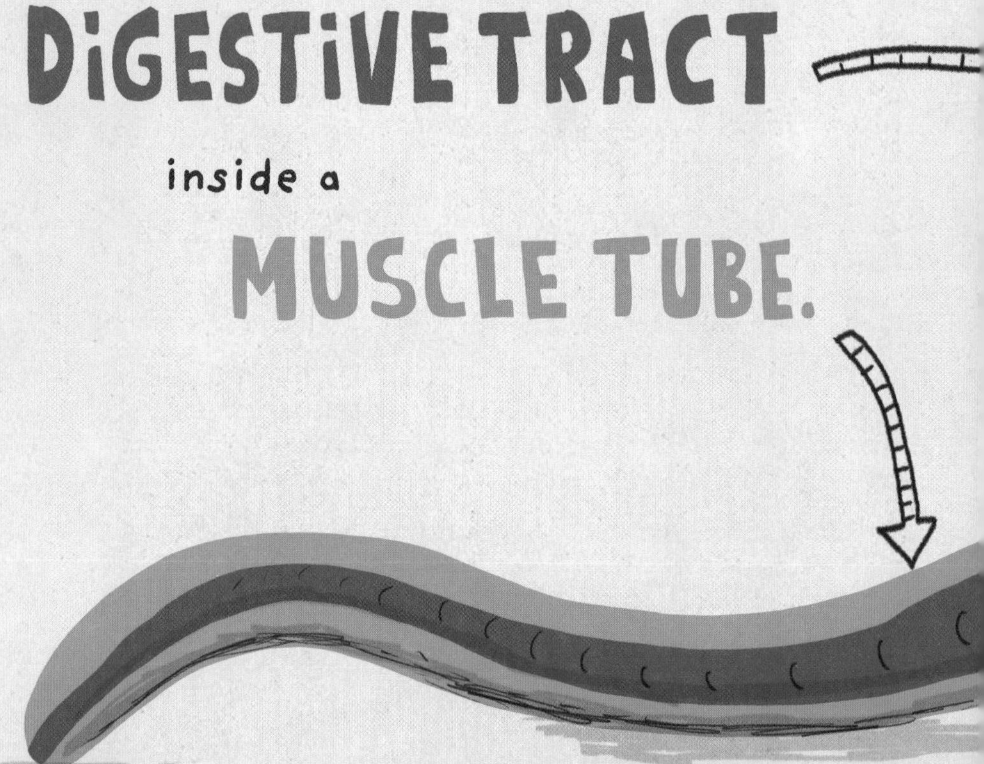

It's that muscle tube that's slimy and disgusting.

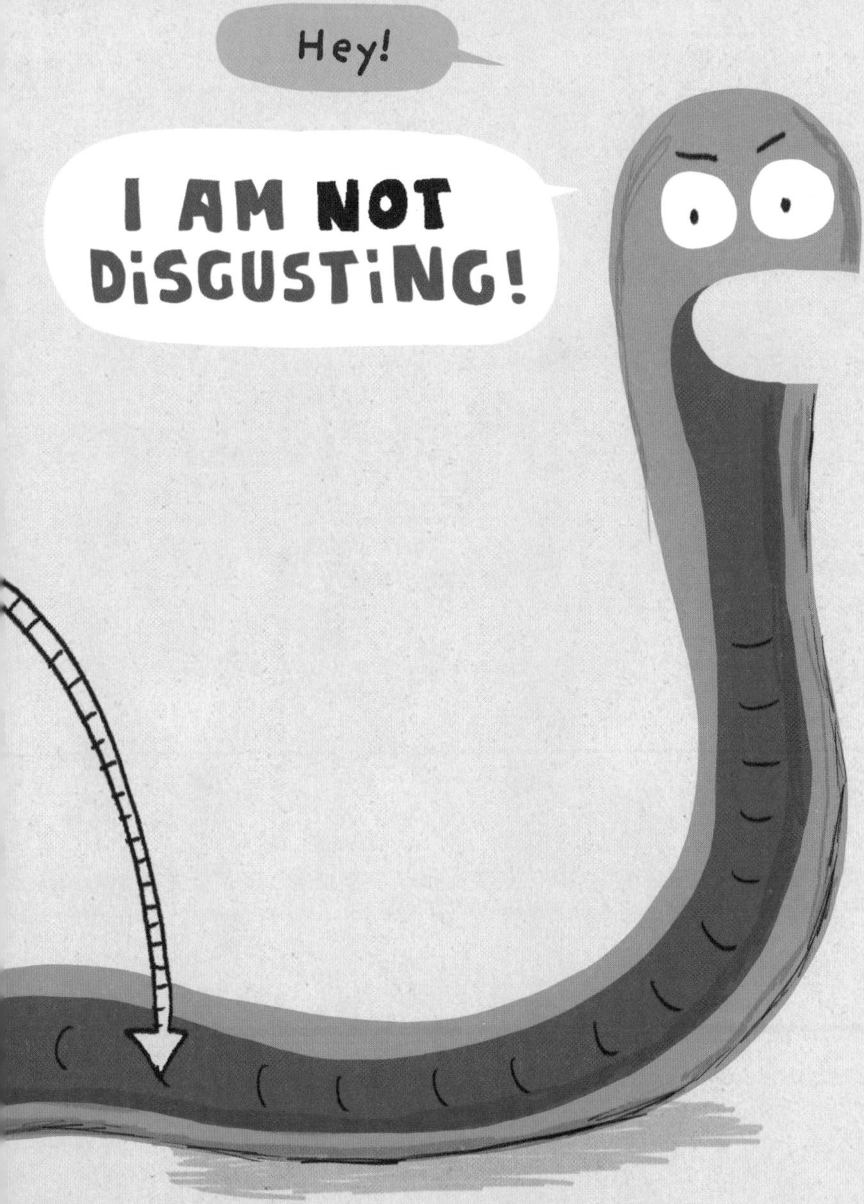

Hey!
I AM NOT DISGUSTING!

Worms have been on earth for

MILLIONS OF YEARS!

Maybe even billions!

Biologists believe they evolved
with the

DiNOSAURS.

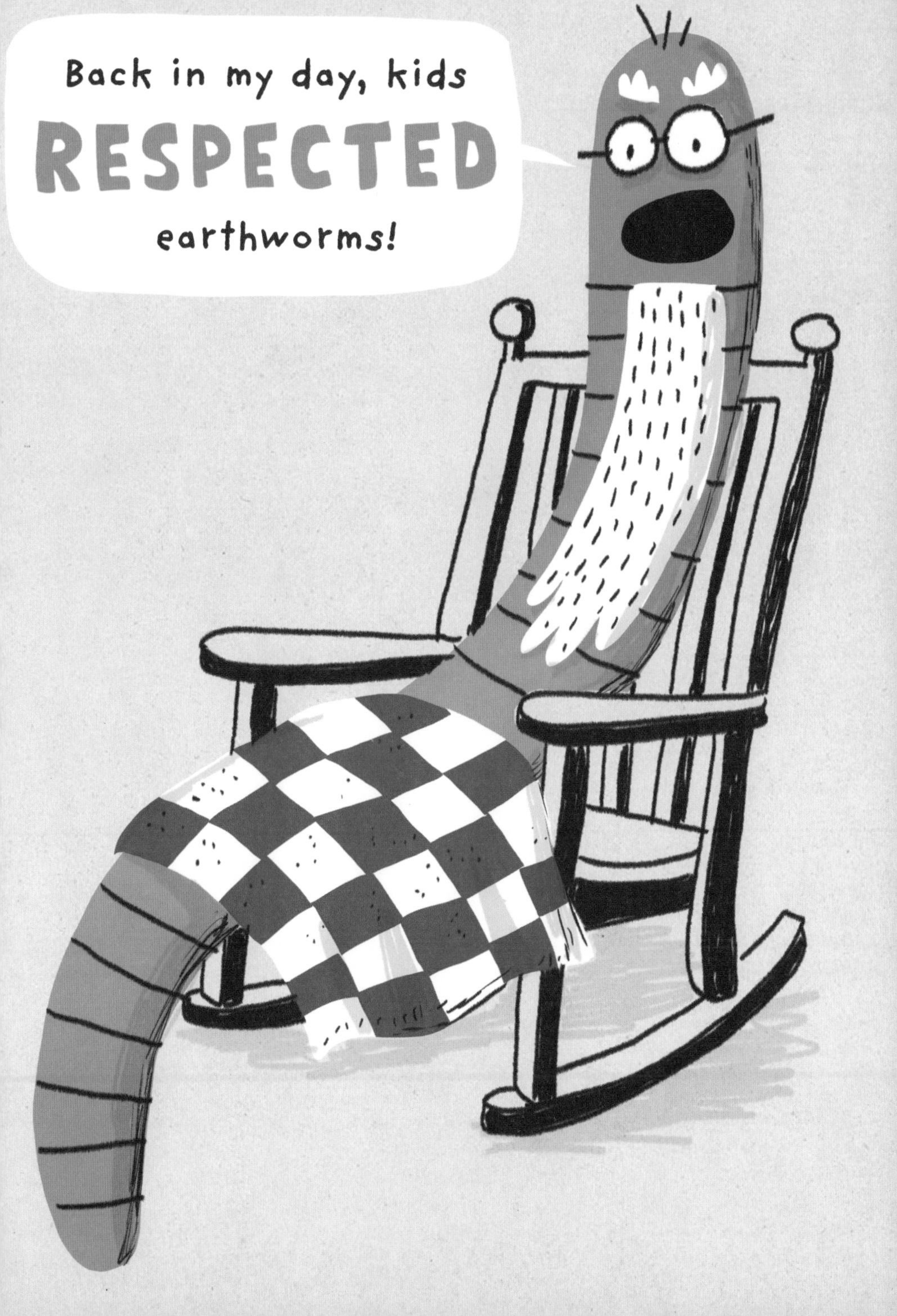
Back in my day, kids RESPECTED earthworms!

Earthworms have

NO EYES,

but they can sense light with something called

PHOTORECEPTORS:

sensors in the worm's skin that react to light.

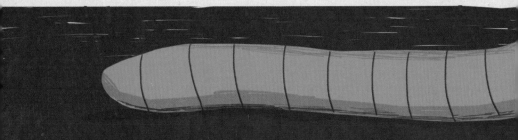

No eyes? That can't be true. I'm sure I had some eyes around here somewhere.
Hmm. Let me look . . .

Earthworms move by

SQUEEZING

their

MUSCLES,

causing their bodies to contract and expand.

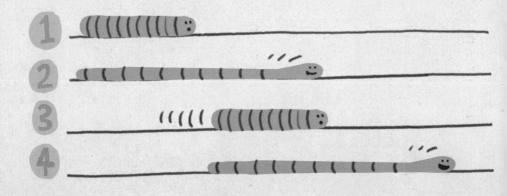

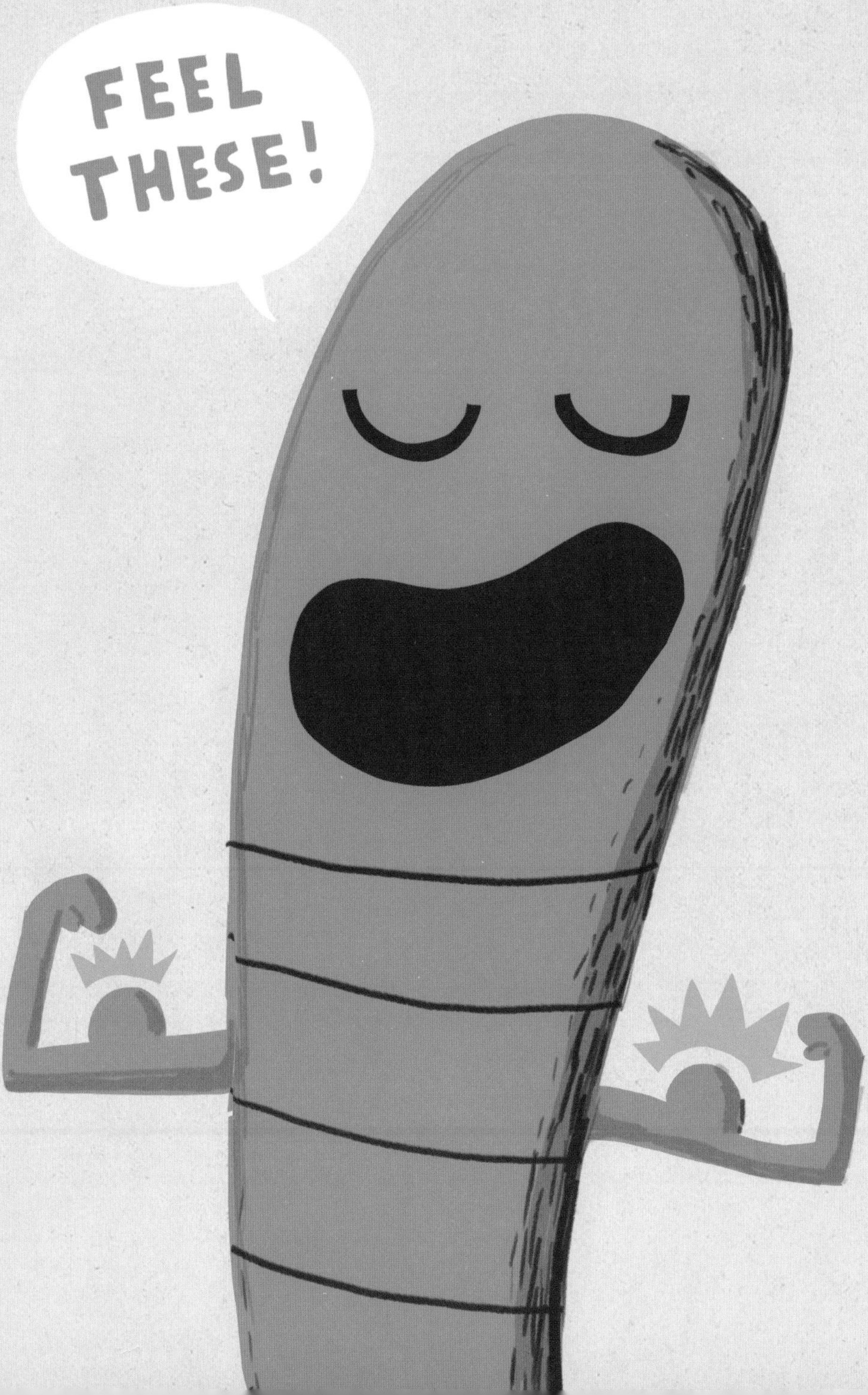
FEEL THESE!

Earthworms eat rotting plants and enrich the soil by making paths that let air and water circulate in it.

IT'S GOOD for NATURE!

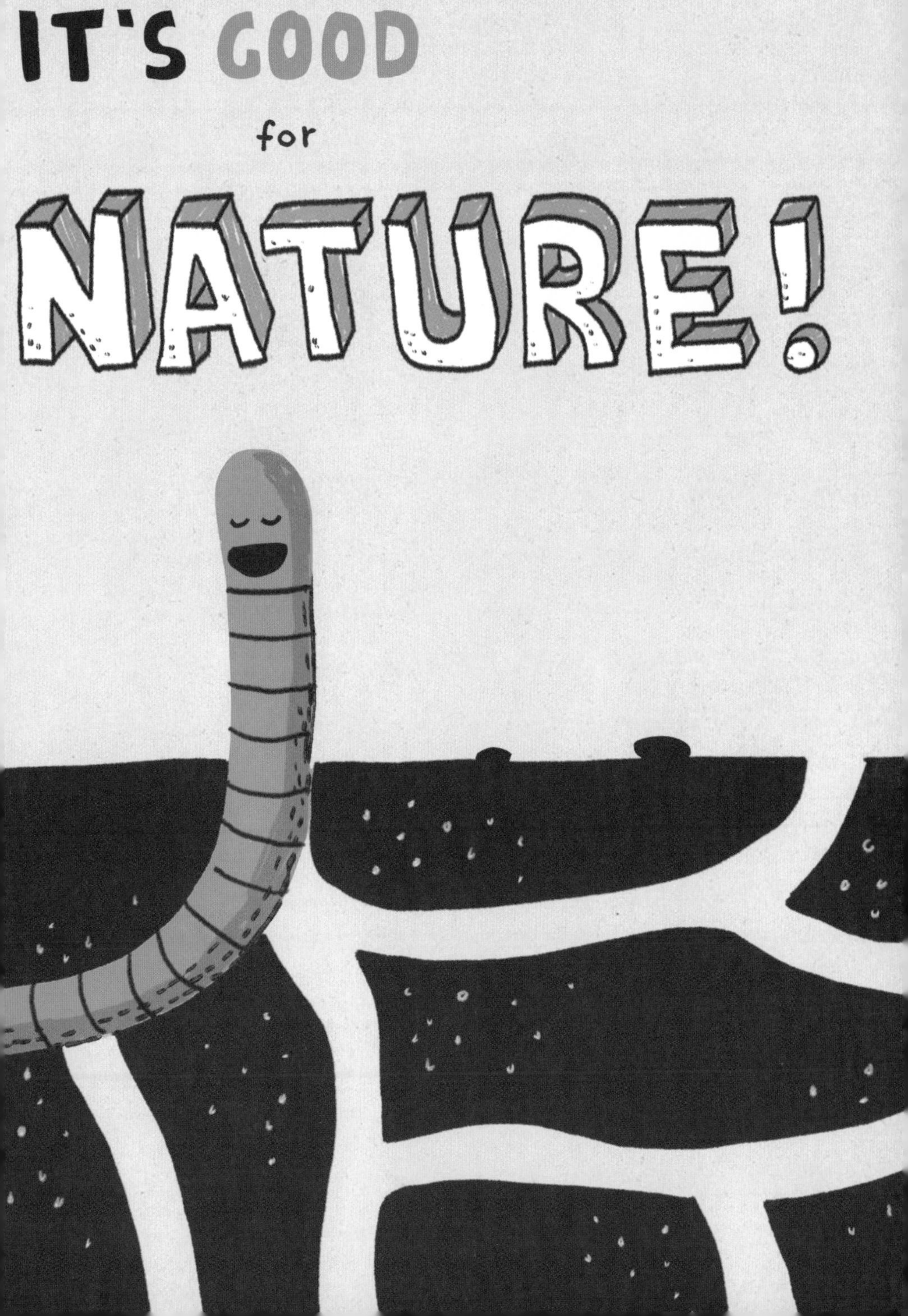

Many kinds of worms are hermaphrodites, which means they have both

MALE

and

FEMALE

reproductive organs.

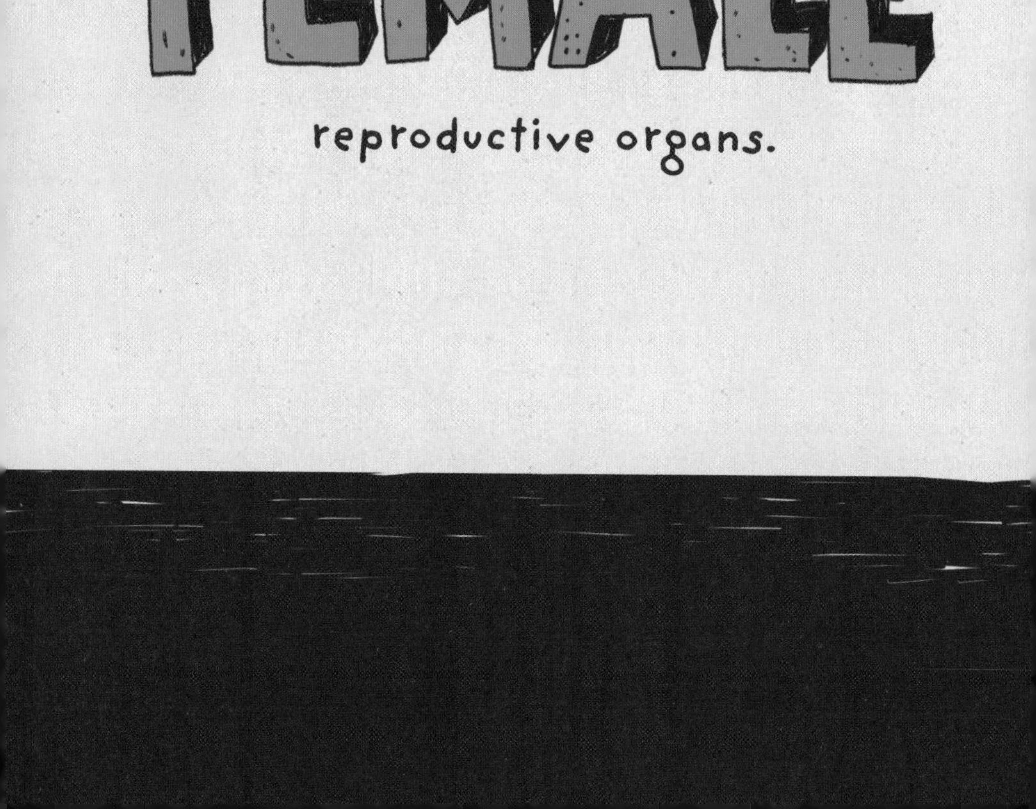

In other words, an earthworm is a boy and a girl at the same time. They still need a partner to reproduce, though.

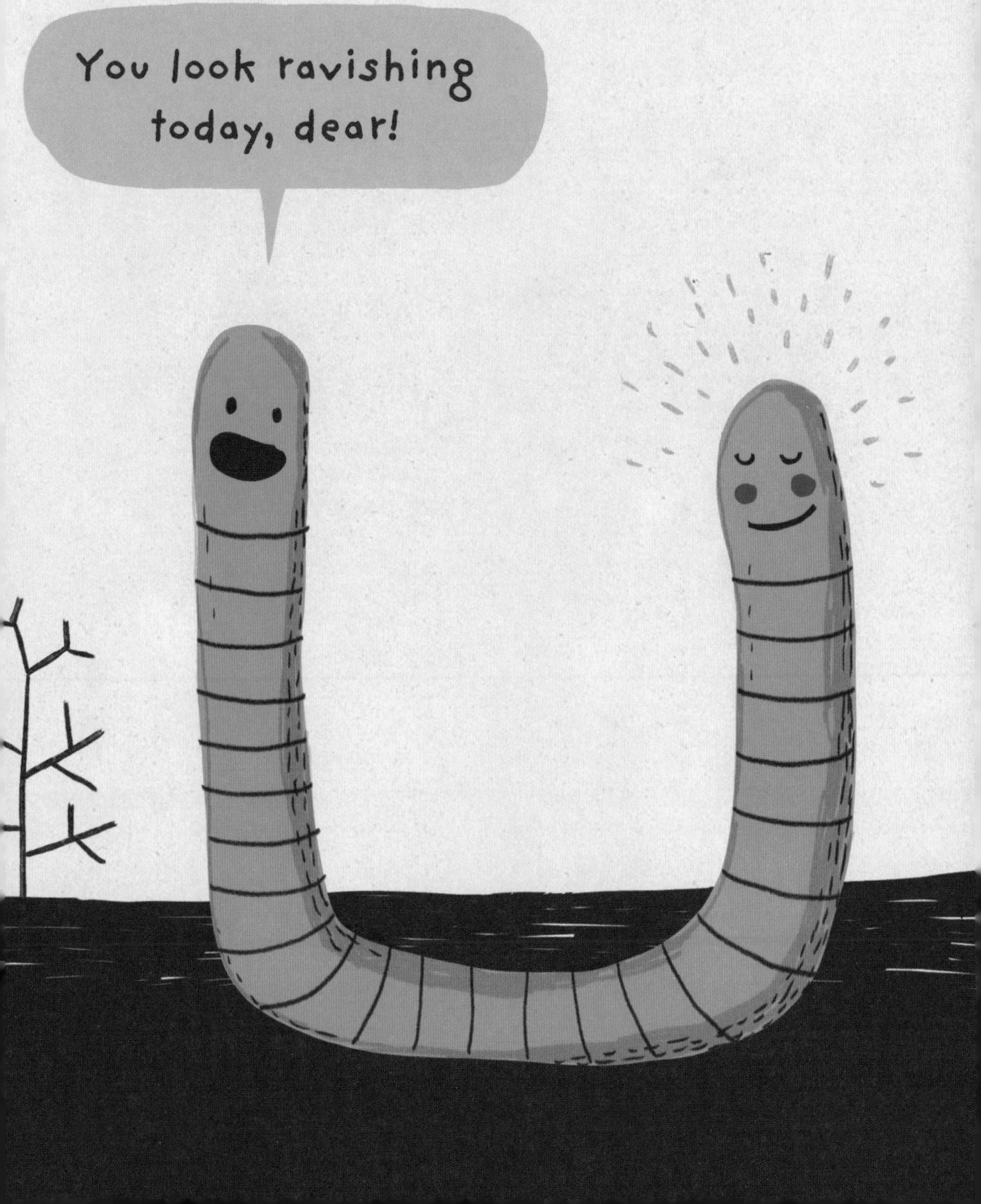
You look ravishing today, dear!

Earthworms might seem

PRETTY GROSS,

but they're very useful! They recycle nature's waste and help turn it into soil. Farmers and gardeners love earthworms!

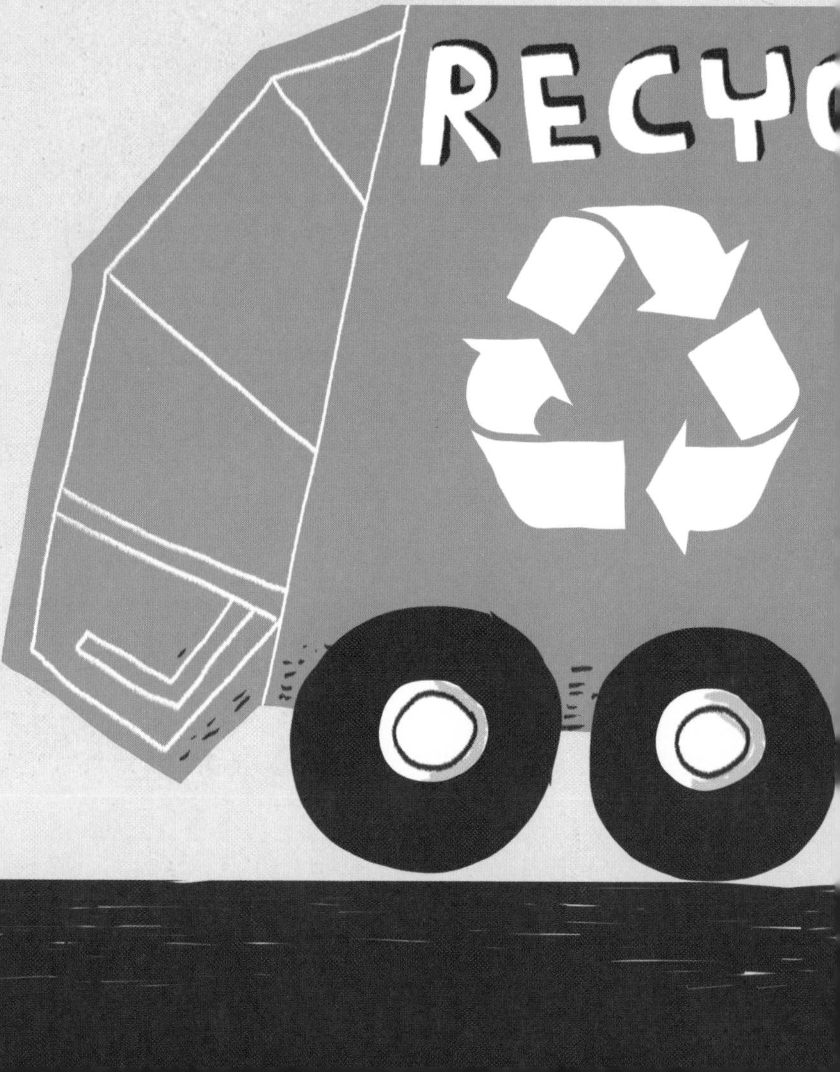
RECYC

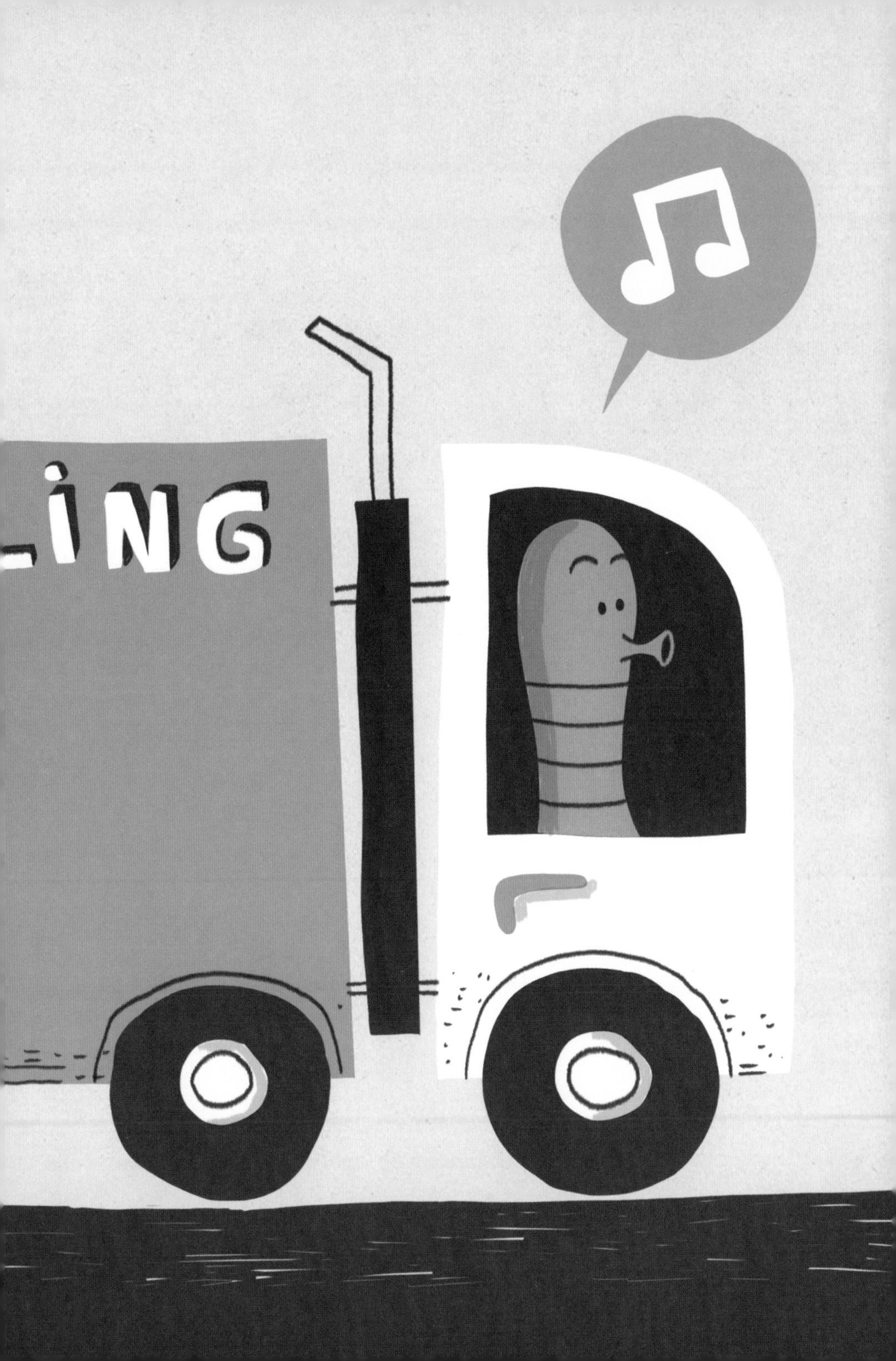
ING

Fishermen use earthworms to catch fish, and some people even eat them and find them

DELICIOUS!

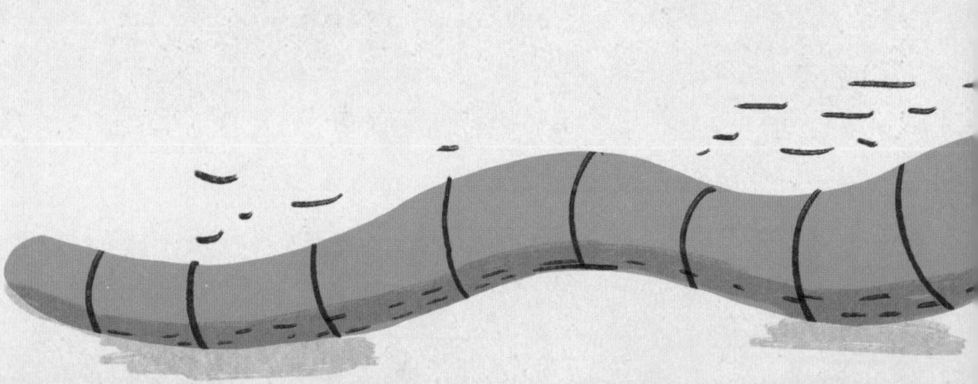

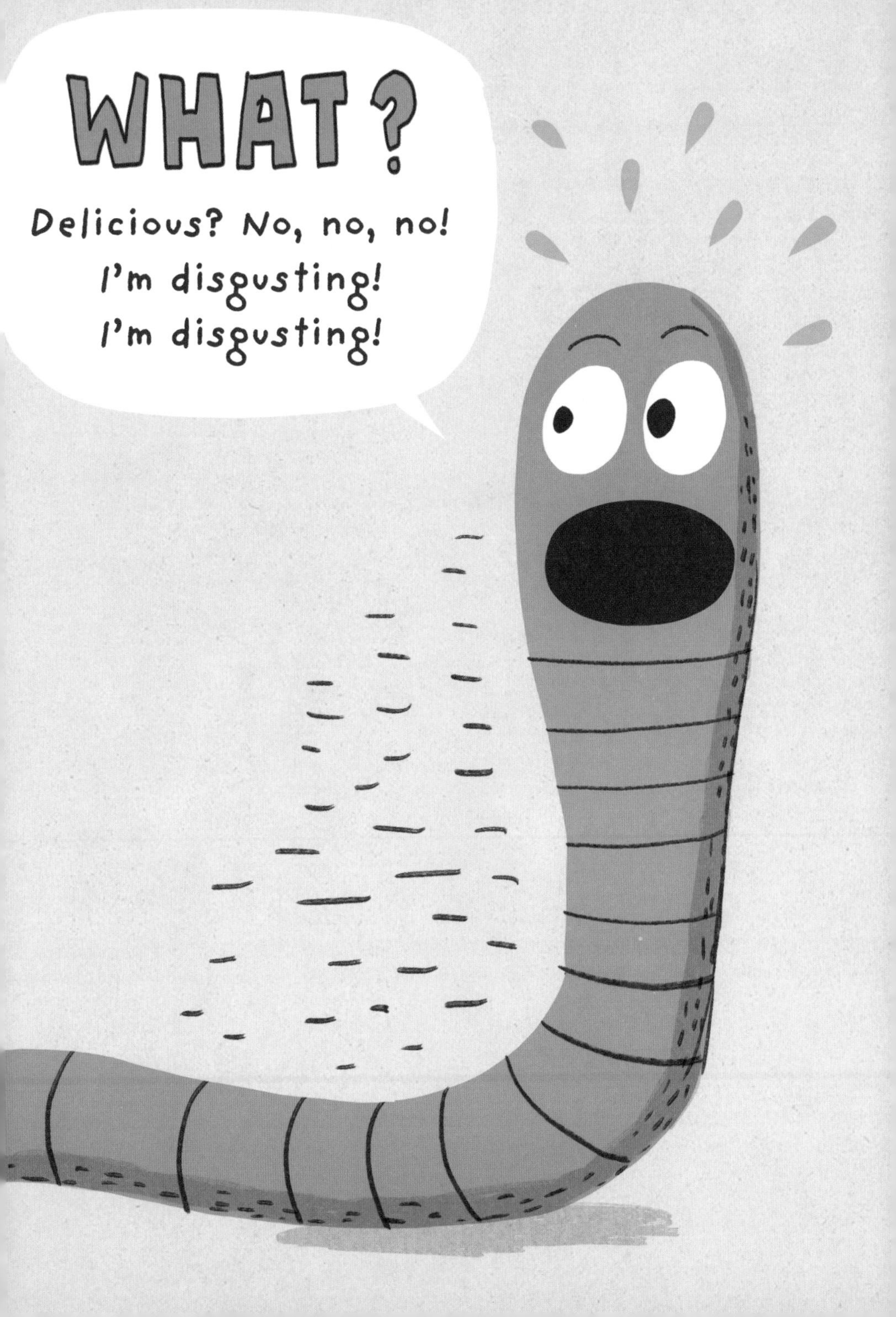
WHAT?
Delicious? No, no, no!
I'm disgusting!
I'm disgusting!

So next time you meet an earthworm, be polite. Worms are

YOUR FRIENDS!

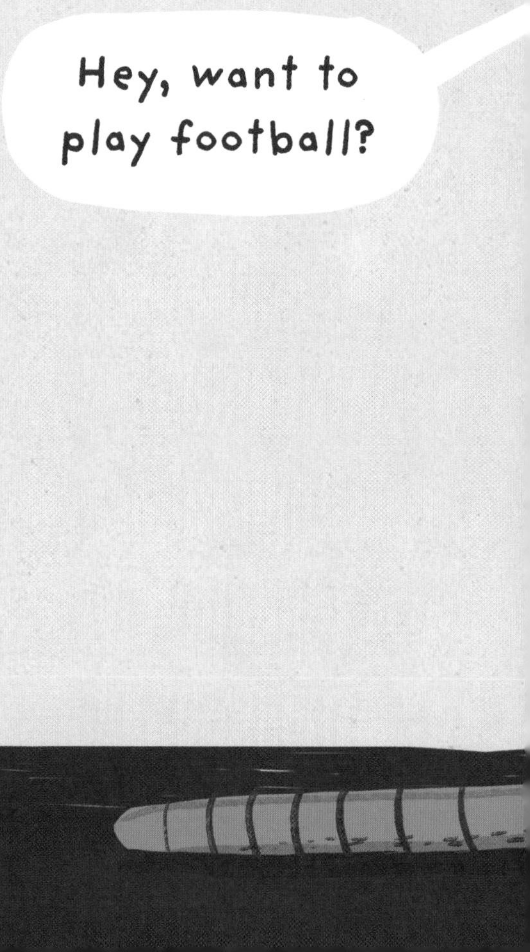

Hey, want to play football?

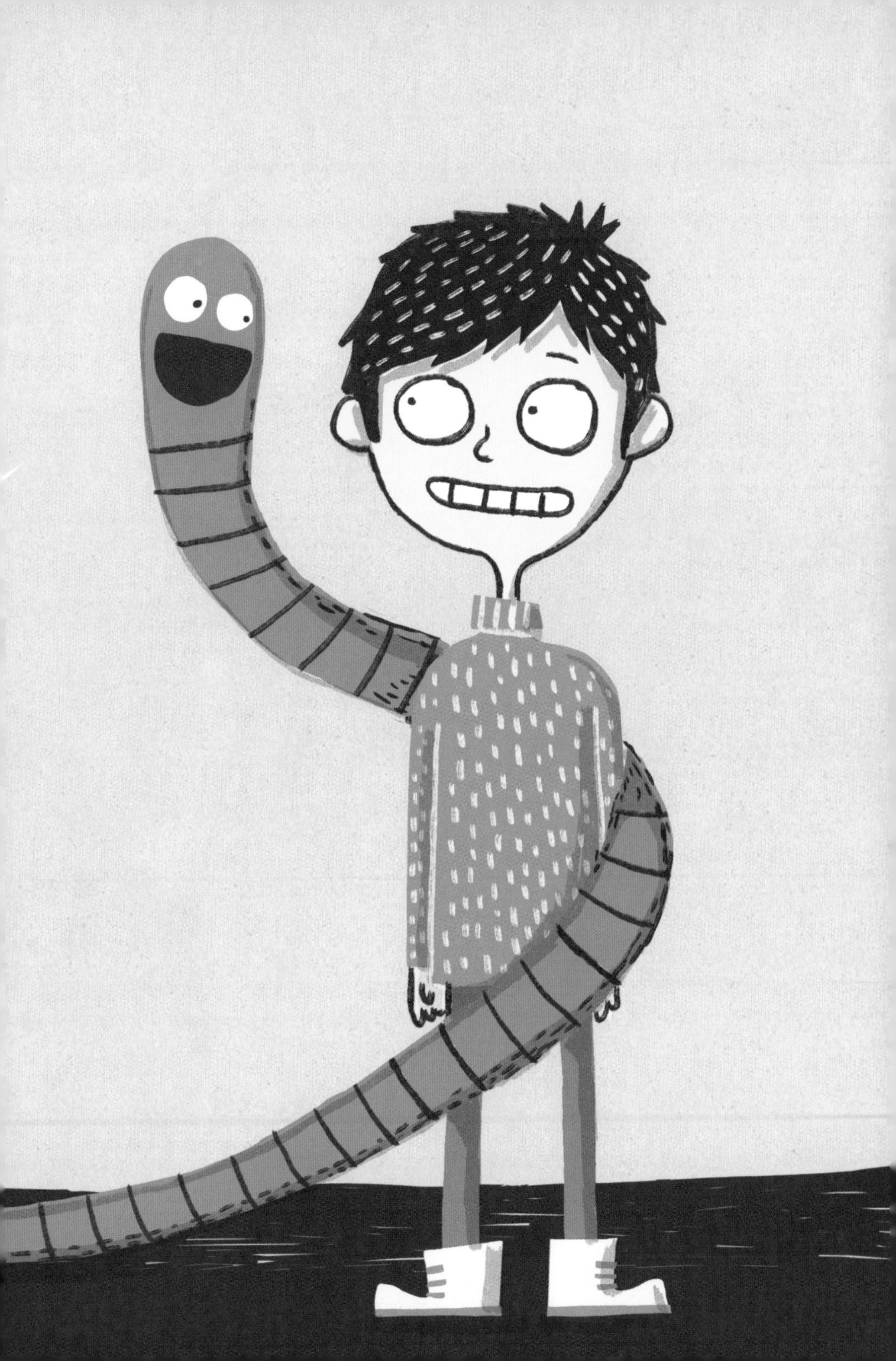

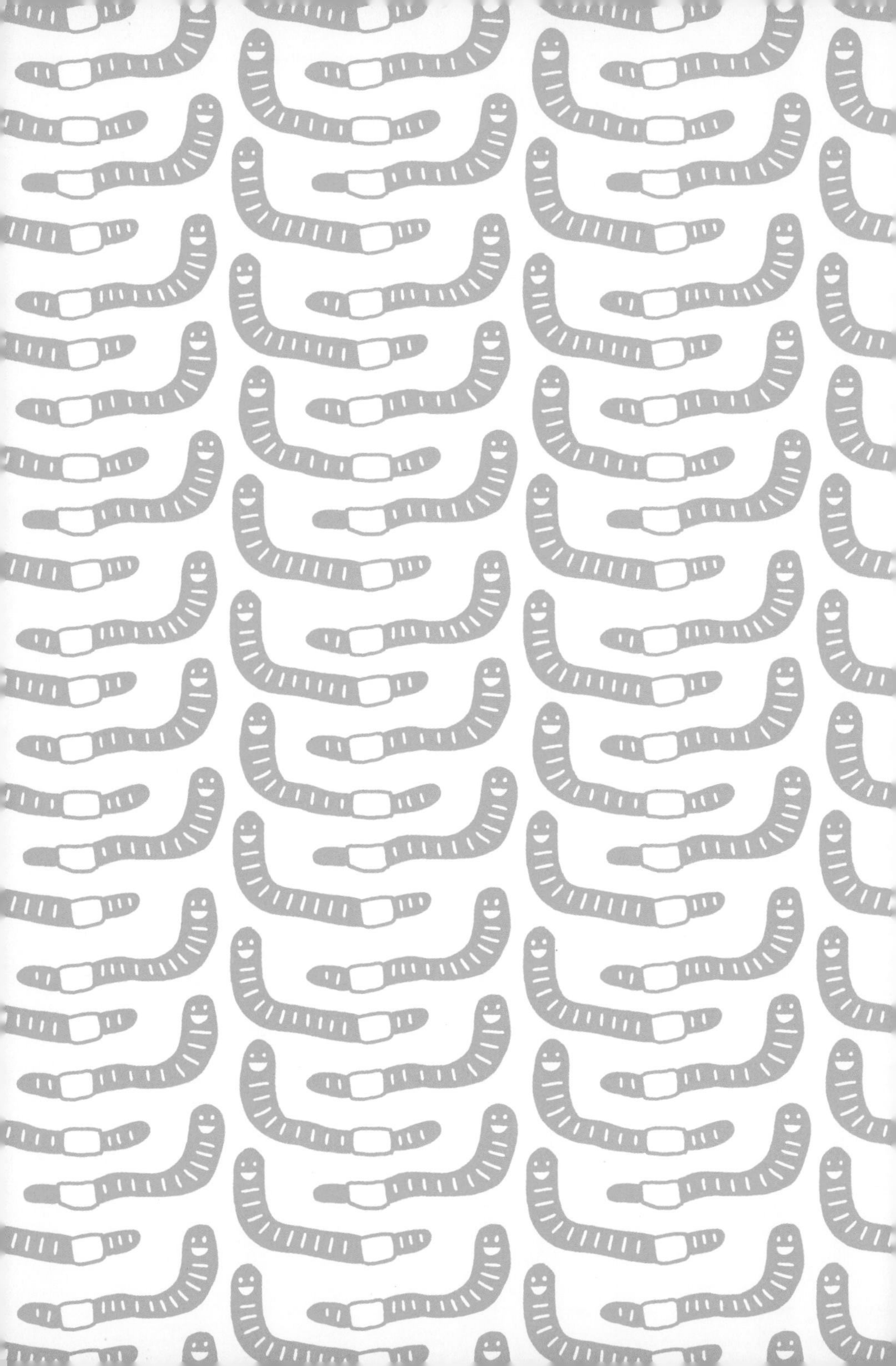